KICK OFF!

WRITTEN BY CLIVE GIFFORD

**ILLUSTRATED BY RICHARD WATSON
AND JULIAN MOSEDALE**

Edited by Helen Brown
Designed by Jack Clucas
Cover design by John Bigwood
Cover artwork by Richard Watson

With special thanks to Jackson and Isaac Clifford
for being brilliant puzzle testers

Buster Books

First published in Great Britain in 2020 by Buster Books,
an imprint of Michael O'Mara Books Limited,
9 Lion Yard, Tremadoc Road, London SW4 7NQ

W www.mombooks.com/buster   f Buster Books   🐦 @BusterBooks

Copyright © Buster Books 2020

A CIP catalogue record for this book is available
from the British Library.

ISBN: 978-1-78055-636-9

2 4 6 8 10 9 7 5 3 1

Papers used by Buster Books are natural, recyclable products made of wood
from well-managed, FSC®-certified forests and other controlled sources.
The manufacturing processes conform to the environmental regulations
of the country of origin.

Printed and bound in February 2020 by CPI Group (UK) Ltd,
108 Beddington Lane, Croydon, CR0 4YY, United Kingdom

MIX
Paper from
responsible sources
FSC
www.fsc.org   FSC® C020471

The facts and records in this book are
accurate to 21 January 2020.

INTRODUCTION

Get your head in the game! This book is full of footie facts and brain games to tackle at your own speed. Read the simple instructions on the page before attacking each puzzle. You may not know all the football trivia needed to complete some puzzles but you can have a guess. Use the answers on pages 112–128 to increase your football knowledge or check your answers. Now, before you kick off, fill in your fact file below.

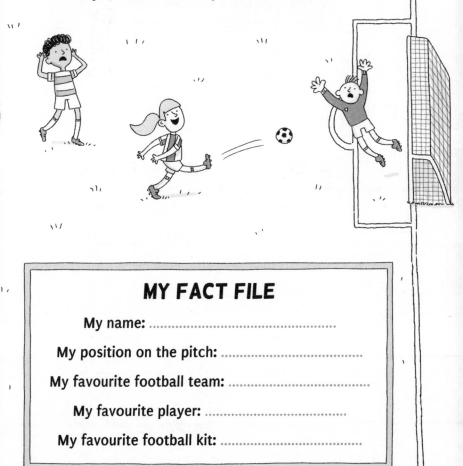

MY FACT FILE

My name: ....

My position on the pitch: ....

My favourite football team: ....

My favourite player: ....

My favourite football kit: ....

TRUE OR FALSE?

Football's a fun sport as some of these silly statements prove. Which ones are true and which ones are false? Tick the box you think is correct.

1. The highest score in the top division of any country was 149-0 in the Madagascan Premier League.

True ☐   False ☐

2. English striker Harry Kane has his forehead insured for £120 million.

True ☐   False ☐

3. A World Cup semi-final in Sweden was abandoned when a herd of moose invaded the pitch.

True ☐   False ☐

4. Denmark failed to qualify for UEFA's 1992 European Championship but ended up winning the tournament.

True ☐   False ☐

5. In 1966, the World Cup trophy was stolen and found over a week later on a street by a dog named Pickles.

True ☐   False ☐

6. Manchester United once signed a defender for a transfer fee of two freezers full of ice cream.

True ☐   False ☐

7. American midfielder Kristine Lilly played 352 times for the US Women's team – more caps than the entire England men's team that started the 2019 Nations League semi-final.

True ☐   False ☐

8. Dutch defender Virgil van Dijk won an Olympic bronze medal in javelin throwing before he turned to football.

True ☐   False ☐

9. When English referee Melvin Sylvester lost his temper during a 1998 game, he showed himself the red card and sent himself off.

True ☐   False ☐

10. English midfielder Dele Alli uses the same shin pads for matches today that he used as an 11-year-old.

True ☐   False ☐

... AND SHE SCORES!

Guide the striker through the football pitch to complete the maze and reach the goal.

FOOTBALL PYRAMIDS

Can you solve the football pyramids?
Each football should contain a number that is
equal to the two footballs immediately beneath it.

WALL BUILDER

Using only two straight lines, build two walls across the area to split each game up into three separate sections. Each section must contain one of each picture. The walls should start at one edge of the area and cross all the way to another edge. Make sure that the walls do not cross over each other.

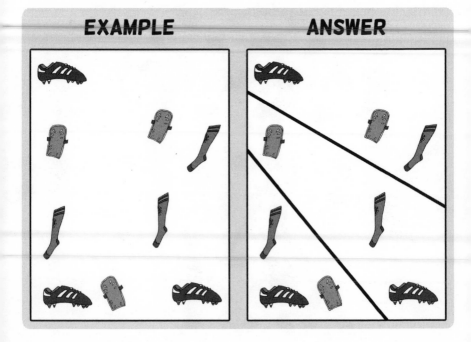

EXAMPLE

ANSWER

GAME ONE

GAME TWO

GAME THREE

GAME FOUR

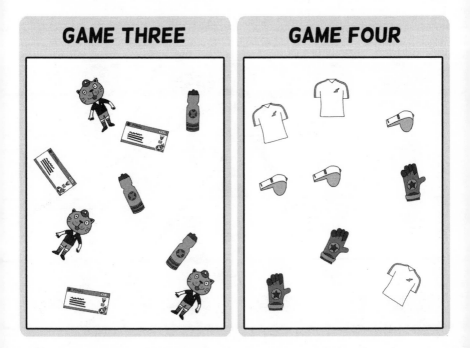

CRAZY CROWDS

Can you spot eight differences between these two football crowds?

CROSSWORD

Put your knowledge of all things football
to the test by completing this crossword.

ACROSS

4. Country of the Lionesses **(7)**

5. Anagram (clue: the boss):
GAENARM **(7)**

7. Animal on the logo
of Leicester City **(3)**

8. Object used by referees for
the first time in 1878 to make
games easier to control **(7)**

DOWN

1. Male football player;
youngest ever England player
at 17 years and 75 days **(4,7)**

2. Kicking the ball from
one of the right angles
of the pitch **(6)**

3. Country with the most
World Cup wins **(6)**

6. Number of players
in a football team **(6)**

DRESSING ROOM COUNTING

How many of the following kit essentials
can you spot in this dressing room?

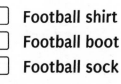
☐ Football shirt
☐ Football boot
☐ Football sock

☐ Bag
☐ Towel
☐ Medal

WORDSEARCH WARM-UP

Can you find these football terms in this wordsearch grid?

```
F  I  S  Q  K  I  O  Y  N  L  R  J  E  V  O  N  U  H  V
O  C  W  F  X  B  Q  H  H  E  Q  V  S  O  A  S  L  D  A
U  P  F  V  P  I  T  C  P  M  C  H  O  D  T  P  E  C  K
L  Q  V  Y  M  A  S  E  V  Z  Q  H  A  J  F  S  R  C  T
F  D  L  Z  K  U  E  T  B  D  A  B  M  N  M  Q  W  Y  I
P  I  A  O  P  K  N  O  I  N  Y  T  F  V  D  O  V  L  H
E  V  N  C  L  D  T  U  C  A  T  T  O  O  W  B  T  J  W
C  L  G  A  Y  D  O  R  Y  F  A  J  P  J  R  D  A  K  B
E  H  O  N  L  M  F  N  C  Q  V  M  W  M  N  W  L  L  L
H  G  S  G  K  T  F  A  L  V  N  A  R  U  H  J  A  A  L
A  L  O  N  U  S  R  M  E  B  D  S  G  B  O  E  M  R  H
L  H  V  L  Y  B  D  E  K  R  A  D  D  F  R  U  W  F  D
F  E  B  A  L  C  Y  N  I  A  M  Z  X  X  I  D  E  G  D
T  N  U  F  C  H  W  T  C  I  E  W  T  D  C  A  F  Y  Q
I  G  K  E  P  V  L  S  K  B  T  V  A  B  S  D  B  M  V
M  F  J  O  D  R  I  B  B  L  E  T  C  A  P  T  A  I  N
E  Y  R  I  D  U  I  H  C  A  S  N  S  D  H  A  X  C  K
T  T  N  L  Q  U  T  G  E  W  K  Z  P  L  C  O  A  C  H
Y  E  L  L  O  W  C  A  R  D  R  E  D  C  A  R  D  C  C
```

BICYCLE KICK
CAPTAIN
COACH
DRIBBLE
FINAL
FORWARD
FOUL
GOALKEEPER

HALF TIME
HANDBALL
RED CARD
SENT OFF
STADIUM
TOURNAMENT
TROPHY
YELLOW CARD

BALL JUMBLE

How many footballs are
jumbled up in this bag?

ODD SHIRT OUT

Can you spot three goalie shirts
that look different to the rest?

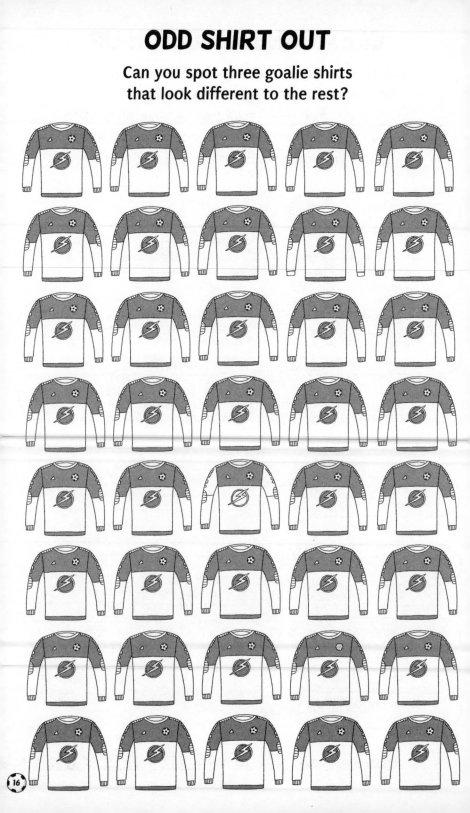

CLEAN SHEET MATCH UP

Goalkeepers crave clean sheets, which is when they finish the game without letting any goals in. The goalkeepers listed below have all broken clean sheet records in different competitions. Can you match the goalie to their stat?

Hope Solo
USA

Joe Hart
England

Peter Shilton
England

Gemma Fay
Scotland

Iker Casillas
Real Madrid

Petr Cech
Chelsea and Arsenal

Edwin van der Sar
Manchester United

Gianluigi Buffon
Juventus

59 clean sheets in UEFA Champions League games (1999–2015)

Most capped goalkeeper in women's football with 203 games and 32 clean sheets for Scotland (1998–2017)

202 clean sheets in 443 Premier League games (2004–2018)

102 clean sheets in women's international games (2000–2016)

46 clean sheets for England in international football (2008–2019)

14 clean sheets in a row in the Premier League (2008–2009)

10 clean sheets at the FIFA World Cup, a joint world record (1982–1990)

53 clean sheets in 123 UEFA Champions League games (2001–2018)

FOOTBALL PHRASES

Unscramble the anagrams to reveal the football terms.

1. CAKB FO HTE NTE

_ _ _ _   _ _

_ _ _   _ _ _

2. YBCCLIE IKKC

_ _ _ _ _ _

_ _ _ _

3. ACELN HSTEE

_ _ _ _ _

_ _ _ _ _

4. EDVI

_ _ _ _

5. GDBRINBLI

_ _ _ _ _ _ _ _

6. NMUEGT

_ _ _ _ _

7. FOF TEH EILN

_ _ _   _ _ _

_ _ _ _

8. ETXAR TMIE

_ _ _ _ _

_ _ _ _

9. OFSEIFD

_ _ _ _ _ _ _

10. RLEOAETIGN

_ _ _ _ _ _ _ _ _ _

SCARF SEQUENCES

Can you solve these four brain chains? Follow each step in order to work out the answer to the sum.

A.

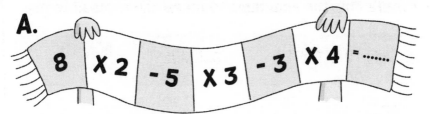

8 × 2 − 5 × 3 − 3 × 4 = ...

B.

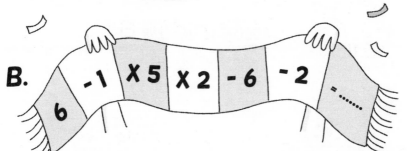

6 − 1 × 5 × 2 − 6 − 2 = ...

C.

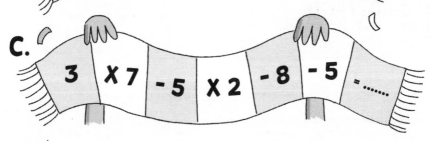

3 × 7 − 5 × 2 − 8 − 5 = ...

D.

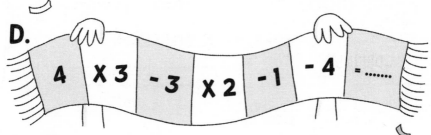

4 × 3 − 3 × 2 − 1 − 4 = ...

GUESS THE GOALS

Can you guess the number of goals scored by these famous goal scorers while they played for the team listed? There are multiple choice options to help you.

LIONEL MESSI BARCELONA
24 321 619

CRISTIANO RONALDO REAL MADRID
450 142 16

ROBERT LEWANDOWSKI BAYERN MUNICH
12 221 824

THIERRY HENRY ARSENAL
228 412 646

ADA HEGERBERG LYON
52 165 216

FRANCESCO TOTTI ROMA
191 307 524

EUSEBIO BENFICA
407 712 999

KRIS BOYD RANGERS
37 138 521

FARA WILLIAMS EVERTON
70 124 612

MARTA UMEÅ IK
90 111 742

PENALTY SHOOTOUT

Can you take your team to goal-scoring glory by only kicking balls that contain multiples of 6 and are next to each other? You can move diagonally.

5	16	2	6	33	16
16	18	24	5	13	4
12	5	11	7	41	45
16	30	42	14	3	13
2	1	3	36	16	31
5	11	6	7	8	10

START

MATCHING CRESTS

Can you match the crest with its twin?
In each square, draw a line to connect
each pair of football crests. The lines
must not cross or touch each other.
Only one line is allowed in each grid
square. You must not use diagonal lines.

EXAMPLE ANSWER

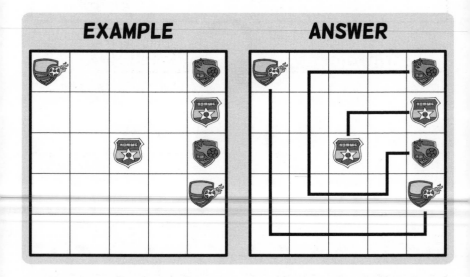

GAME ONE GAME TWO

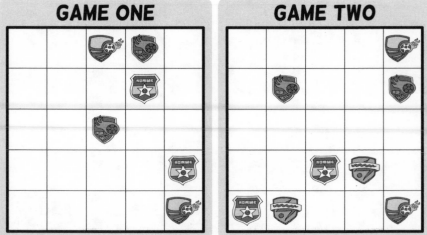

GAME THREE

GAME FOUR

GAME FIVE

GAME SIX

GAME SEVEN

GAME EIGHT

EUROPA LEAGUE TEAMS

Can you find these Europa League and UEFA cup winning teams in this wordsearch grid?

```
F E Y E N O O R D V A L E N C I A B F
X X N I X F H C S Q F K M K U A O J B
N N Z E N I T S T P E T E R S B U R G
T M R Z H J J C P Y V Y J N U A R D B
D A L R Q R R A K B Z V G J E S I I A
A N Q R J J F M V M M R T S S R E R Y
Q C C I W N R A X J P Z L D D N E U E
J H J O G Z J S V Q I E X A C T F O R
O E L S Y A U B E C H P M E N U T M N
R S J Q E T L V B C D O V I B R S H M
W T I Y N E N A W L C X C A O G E K U
L E X E L E M Z T I I H L P R T V K N
R R V U H R V U T A A V C S N R I Z I
W U K R A Y Q E F J S B E T G L L D C
J N W P T Q L I D R C A R R H N L Z H
T I Z Y O T Z F Q P S O R Q P I A F N
P T Q F A K S T K L C F W A F O M Z Y
J E S C S K A M O S C O W J Y Q O A C
K D S H A K H T A R D O N E T S K L T
```

ATLETICO MADRID
BAYERN MUNICH
CHELSEA
CSKA MOSCOW
PORTO
FEYENOORD
GALATASARAY
INTER

JUVENTUS
LIVERPOOL
MANCHESTER UNITED
PARMA
SEVILLA
SHAKHTAR DONETSK
VALENCIA
ZENIT ST PETERSBURG

FOOTBALL PAIRS

Draw horizontal and vertical lines to join pairs of footballs so that each pair contains one white football and one shaded football. Lines cannot cross over each other or cross over footballs. Each football must form part of one pair only.

EXAMPLE

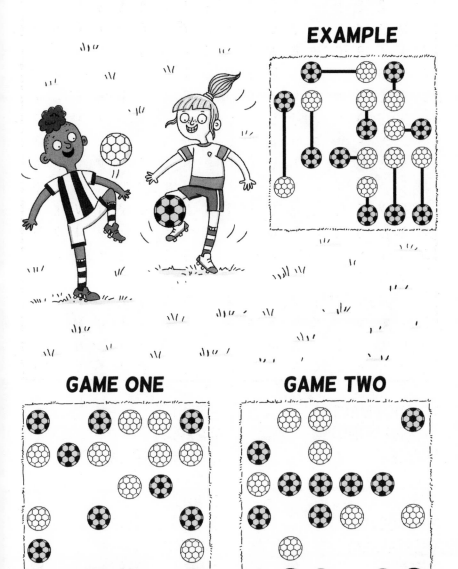

GAME ONE

GAME TWO

FOOTBALL MAZE

Find your way through this football
to reach the middle of the maze.

CROSSWORD

Put your knowledge of all things football
to the test by completing this crossword.

ACROSS

1. Country that hosted the
first Women's World Cup **(5)**
4. Dog that found the World
Cup trophy in 1966 **(7)**
6. Colour of Wales'
international home shirts **(3)**
7. Country that won the first
FIFA World Cup in 1930 **(7)**

DOWN

1. An instructor, or trainer **(5)**
2. Female American
goalkeeper; played for
the national team from
2000 to 2016 **(4,4)**
3. Anagram (clue: position on
the pitch): DNFEERDE **(8)**
5. The Gunners **(7)**

WHO AM I?

Can you work out the identity of these famous footballers from the clues provided below?

1. I was born in Marseille, France and played my first match of professional football at the age of 17. My nickname is 'Zizou'. Who am I?

2. I am an England women's team defender who has twice won the UEFA Women's Champions League with French club Lyon. My surname is the same colour as the medal I received with England at the 2015 Women's World Cup. Who am I?

3. I am Real-Madrid's all-time leading goal scorer with 451 goals in 438 appearances. Who am I?

4. I have played over 140 times for England as a midfielder and have won the Women's Super League with Manchester City in 2016. I am nicknamed 'Crouchy' by my teammates as I am tall. Who am I?

5. I have scored 162 Premier League goals including the most by a substitute. In 2009, I scored five goals for Tottenham Hotspur in just one half of a match. Who am I?

6. I scored my 12th Premier League hat-trick in 2020, beating Alan Shearer's record of 11. I have also scored an average of 30 goals in all competitions for 6 seasons in a row including 2018–2019. Who am I?

7. I played for Chelsea Ladies and Leeds Carnegie before scoring 23 goals in 26 matches for Birmingham City. I moved to Manchester City in 2019. I have played over 80 times for England as a forward and appeared at both the 2011 and 2019 Women's World Cup. Who am I?

8. I scored 17 Premier League goals for three teams, Crystal Palace, Aston Villa and Middlesbrough, before becoming England team manager in 2016. Who am I?

9. I have made 25 appearances at World Cups which is more than any other player in the world. Who am I?

10. I'm a tall striker who has played for seven different Premier League clubs, including Tottenham Hotspur, Liverpool and Stoke City, as well as scoring 22 goals for England. Who am I?

FOOTBALL JOKES: FIRST HALF

What do Sergio Aguero and a magician have in common?

They're both good at hat tricks.

Which famous footballer has an untidy bedroom?

Lionel Messi

Football fan 1: "Why do they call the new manager 'Public Transport'?"

Football fan 2: "Because he loves to train and coach!"

What is the name of a storm that also scores lots of goals?

A Harrykane

Which football team do ghosts support?

Liver-ghoul

How do football managers
stay cool during a hot match?

They stand near the fans.

Which fairytale character is
a rubbish football player?

*Cinderella because she always
runs away from the ball!*

Who saves the football when a
team of ghosts play a match?

The Ghoul-keeper

Referee: "I will have to abandon
the game — the pitch is flooded."

Manager: "Don't worry. I'll bring on my subs!"

Which team do German cats support?

Bayern Mew-nich

BACK OF THE NET

Follow the lines to find out which
footballer scored the goal.

JOSH

MAE

ELLEN

GARY

MYSTERY CREST

Connect the dots to reveal a
Premier League club crest.

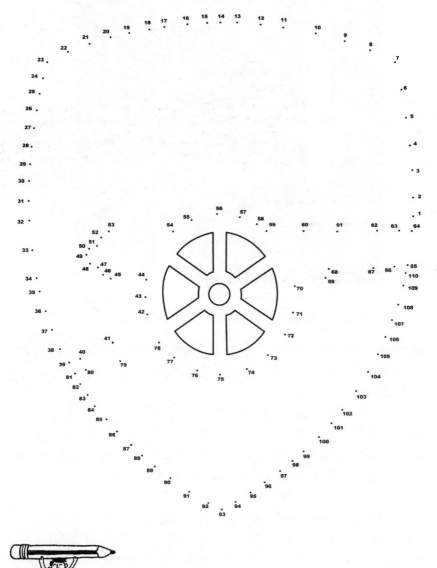

CROSSWORD

Put your knowledge of all things football
to the test by completing this crossword.

ACROSS

3. Number of lions on the England team badge **(5)**

6. Winners of the 2016 Premier League **(9,4)**

7. Nickname is 'Il Polpo', which translates to 'the Octopus' **(4,5)**

8. A shot or pass made with the head **(6)**

DOWN

1. Winner of the 2019 Fifa Women's World Cup Golden Boot **(5,7)**

2. Occupying a position on the pitch where playing the ball is not allowed **(7)**

4. First player to score 100 goals for Spurs in the Premier League **(5,4)**

5. Football position; a person who cleans a floor or road **(7)**

CHAMPIONS LEAGUE TEAMS

Can you find these Champions League and European Cup winners in this wordsearch grid?

```
X B H F O A F A M A R S E I L L E Q A
M O O X W A Q B A Y E R N M U N I C H
A D L R P B J B G V D O B H Z D I L L
N P T I U F Y C A Y U M E K N F I L A
C T O O V S L J F R S D W P N J C F C
H E W R E E S J F H C Q F E S Y I T M
E J M Y D V R I U K U E B U D Z O X I
S M L P H A B P A V L P L C G I H Y L
T R U O E Z F R O D E E T O Z H M K A
E C E D V T J M A O O N V J N O F Q N
R E Q A W L V Y J A L R T Z U A J A X
U Z T U L T P J L H A T T U S W T C Q
N I P O A M B U F R F L I M S T I V C
I N T E R L A A I O N A L E U T O D H
T M H B A K H D W P J U Z H L N N D E
E Z R Z Q W H W R X O Q O E X D D C L
D Q N K C C K Z T X I F R C Z H W H B S
V B X Q R T F S C L D K T F F X V F E
H A M B U R G E M I D A N O E J I O A
```

AJAX
BARCELONA
BAYERN MUNICH
BENFICA
BORUSSIA DORTMUND
CELTIC
CHELSEA
HAMBURG

INTER
JUVENTUS
LIVERPOOL
MANCHESTER UNITED
MARSEILLE
AC MILAN
PORTO
REAL MADRID

CLUB CONUNDRUM

Unscramble the names of these famous clubs and then draw a line to connect them to their home stadiums.

LEAR ADDRIM

VIREOLPOL

LEANCOBRA

ANYBER UNCHIM

ERRSNAG

CA NMAIL

ASMELLIER

SHELACE

SANTIAGO BERNABÉU

ANFIELD

CAMP NOU

ALLIANZ ARENA

SAN SIRO

STAMFORD BRIDGE

STADE VELODROME

IBROX

IT'S A GOAL!

Spot eight differences between these
two penalty shootout scenes.

FOOTBALL LEGENDS QUIZ

Some footballers become more than famous – they become icons of the sport. Can you answer these multiple choice questions about these football legends?

1. In 1959, Brazilian centre-forward Pelé scored 127 goals for Santos in one season, and won the World Cup three times for Brazil. How many hat-tricks has he scored in total?

a) 11

b) 27

c) 41

d) 92

2. Which team did English midfielder David Beckham score his first League goal for in 1995?

a) Manchester United

b) Preston North End

c) LA Galaxy

d) West Ham United

3. American midfielder Mia Hamm scored 158 goals and made 145 assists for the US national team in her career. How old was she when she made her debut for the US national team?

a) 15

b) 17

c) 19

d) 21

4. Russian goalkeeper Lev Yashin was the only goalkeeper to win the Ballon D'Or for the best footballer in the world. How many penalties did he manage to save?

a) 41

b) 78

c) 150

d) 243

5. German striker Miroslav Klose has scored more goals at World Cup tournaments than any other player. How many goals has he scored?

a) 12

b) 16

c) 20

d) 32

6. Italian legend, Paolo Maldini played 902 games in 25 seasons, all for which Italian club?

a) AC Milan

b) Napoli

c) Roma

d) Inter Milan

7. In 2015, American forward Carli Lloyd became the first female footballer to score a hat-trick in a World Cup final, all scored within the first 16 minutes of the game. Who was Carli's team playing?

a) Germany

b) England

c) France

d) Japan

8. Which Scottish football icon played more games (102) for his country than any other and is the joint-leading goal scorer with 30 goals?

a) Denis Law

b) Kenny Miller

c) Kenny Dalglish

d) Ally McCoist

9. English midfielder Bobby Charlton played over 750 matches for Manchester United and 106 games for England, during which time he helped win the World Cup. How many times throughout his career was he booked?

a) 2

b) 11

c) 24

d) 40

10. Canadian women's football legend Christine Sinclair scored a goal against England in 2019. Which milestone did she reach in her goals for Canada?

a) 50th goal

b) 100th goal

c) 120th goal

d) 180th goal

FOOTIE LEGENDS

Unscramble the anagrams to reveal
some legends of the game.

1. LNIEOL SESIM

_ _ _ _ _ _

_ _ _ _ _

2. MRAAT

_ _ _ _ _

3. CRTIISAON OOANRLD

_ _ _ _ _ _ _ _ _

_ _ _ _ _ _ _

4. PLEERILN HDERAR

_ _ _ _ _ _ _ _

_ _ _ _ _ _

5. MENARY

_ _ _ _ _ _

6. NWYAE OORYEN

_ _ _ _ _

_ _ _ _ _ _

7. IEDZEINN IANDEZ

_ _ _ _ _ _ _ _

_ _ _ _ _ _

8. DIDAV EAKHBMC

_ _ _ _ _

_ _ _ _ _ _ _

9. MAS RKER

_ _ _

_ _ _ _

10. DAA RGHEREBGE

_ _ _

_ _ _ _ _ _ _ _

FOOTBALL SHIRT PAIRING

Draw lines to match up the
pairs of identical shirts.

FOOTIE FACT MATCH UP

Below are six sets of lists. Each word in the left-hand
list can be matched with a word on the right-hand list.
Match all the words until they are all paired up.

1. Can you pair up the mascots to their club?

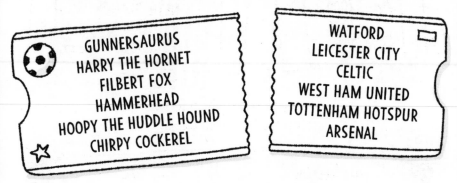

GUNNERSAURUS
HARRY THE HORNET
FILBERT FOX
HAMMERHEAD
HOOPY THE HUDDLE HOUND
CHIRPY COCKEREL

WATFORD
LEICESTER CITY
CELTIC
WEST HAM UNITED
TOTTENHAM HOTSPUR
ARSENAL

2. Match the men's World Cup year with the
country in which the tournament was held.

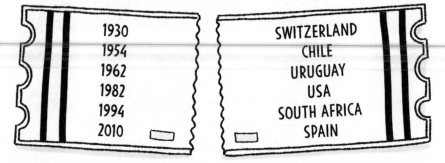

1930
1954
1962
1982
1994
2010

SWITZERLAND
CHILE
URUGUAY
USA
SOUTH AFRICA
SPAIN

3. Can you pair up the name of a famous club
with what the club was originally called?

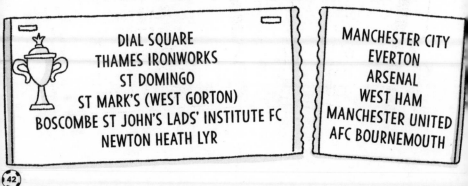

DIAL SQUARE
THAMES IRONWORKS
ST DOMINGO
ST MARK'S (WEST GORTON)
BOSCOMBE ST JOHN'S LADS' INSTITUTE FC
NEWTON HEATH LYR

MANCHESTER CITY
EVERTON
ARSENAL
WEST HAM
MANCHESTER UNITED
AFC BOURNEMOUTH

4. Match the country to the year they last won the UEFA European Championship.

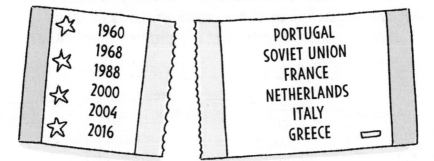

☆ 1960	PORTUGAL
☆ 1968	SOVIET UNION
☆ 1988	FRANCE
☆ 2000	NETHERLANDS
2004	ITALY
☆ 2016	GREECE

5. Do you know which football star plays for which country?

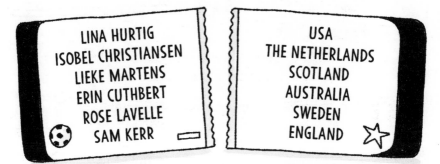

LINA HURTIG	USA
ISOBEL CHRISTIANSEN	THE NETHERLANDS
LIEKE MARTENS	SCOTLAND
ERIN CUTHBERT	AUSTRALIA
ROSE LAVELLE	SWEDEN
SAM KERR	ENGLAND

6. Match the club to the year they won the FA Cup final. Some of the earliest final winners aren't teams you find in the Premier League today.

1872	OXFORD UNIVERSITY
1874	BLACKPOOL
1882	OLD ETONIANS
1953	WANDERERS
2013	MANCHESTER CITY
2019	WIGAN ATHLETIC

PREMIER LEAGUE QUIZ

Since the Premier League formed in 1992, it has been full of thrills, spills and lots of goals. Can you score highly in this multiple choice quiz?

1. Which team let in the first Premier League goal in 1992, scored by Brian Deane?

a) Arsenal

b) Blackburn Rovers

c) Manchester United

d) Ipswich Town

2. Who scored 24 Premier League goals to help his team win the championship in 2015-2016?

a) Sergio Aguero

b) Jamie Vardy

c) Romelu Lukaku

d) Eden Hazard

3. Which Premier League team did Tottenham Hotspur beat 9-1 in the 2009-2010 season?

a) Wigan Athletic

b) Portsmouth

c) Bolton Wanderers

d) Aston Villa

4. Between 2004 and 2008, which Premier League team went 86 games in a row without losing at their home ground?

a) Stoke City

b) West Ham United

c) Manchester United

d) Chelsea

5. A real fox in the box – which striker has scored all 53 of his Premier League goals from inside the area?

a) Pierre-Emerick Aubameyang

b) Javier Hernandez

c) Alvaro Morata

d) Glenn Murray

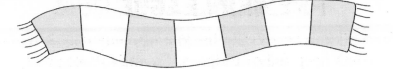

6. Which striker has scored the most goals with their head in the Premier League?

a) Didier Drogba

b) Peter Crouch

c) Harry Kane

d) Wayne Rooney

7. Which manager has managed a record 828 Premier League games?

a) José Mourinho

b) Sir Alex Ferguson

c) Arséne Wenger

d) Rafa Benitez

8. In 2002, which 16-year-old player became the then youngest Premier League goalscorer for Leeds United? In 2018, he played his 500th Premier League match.

a) James Milner

b) Gareth Barry

c) Robbie Fowler

d) Aaron Lennon

9. Which Premier League team went unbeaten for a whole season in 2003–2004?

a) Manchester United

b) Everton

c) Chelsea

d) Arsenal

10. Aston Villa and Manchester City defender Richard Dunne holds the Premier League record for the most own goals. How many own goals has he scored?

a) 6

b) 10

c) 14

d) 33

NICKNAME SEARCH

Can you find these team nicknames in this wordsearch grid? Do you know what teams they belong to?

```
C I T I Z E N S U M T F T I G E R S C
Z I Q C V R U U Y H A J Q X P E Y I L
Y Y S Z O H W I W M E N C J Z F R B A
V D B S D Y M I G J S X T P W D I W R
H U I P T O F F E E S T W X K S G O E
U G R M O C I X A B A G G I E S D B T
Y P E Z U S N N G F E Q O N A U E H S
C E D L Y K D I C M P M S H H Z S U P
O Z S W U D R S V S Z R K X K E D T J
C Q R X Y E U Y P Y E V I L L A I N S
N G C A E H S O Q N B U W G Y B M R G
T Y P X B R O G N S C A A S U J B G F
Z N O V E H B U R Y U E N Z A S F Q O
A O E T R W G E R V C A J T E I K C X
X C T E Y D M B U M W A B I A Y N B E
E O P U A M I M L S N V G Y A G Q T S
P U J B A K R B H U H D D B N L H W S
S Y V H N V I G C N E I N A O Q B E N
R M L W P A C U L J R S M Y V O C R U
```

BAGGIES	POTTERS
BLUES	REDS
CITIZENS	SAINTS
CLARETS	SUPER HOOPS
EAGLES	SWANS
FOXES	TOFFEES
GUNNERS	TIGERS
HAMMERS	VILLAINS

... AND HE SCORES!

Guide the striker through the football pitch to complete the maze and reach the goal.

COMPLEX CUBE

Imagine cutting out and folding up the picture below to make a cube. Which one of the four images at the bottom of the page would match that cube? A good way to tackle this puzzle is to first work out which cubes are clearly wrong. The remaining cube must be the correct one.

A.

B.

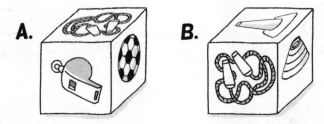

C.

D.

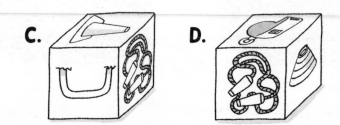

STADIUM SILHOUETTES

Can you match each stadium to its silhouette?

1.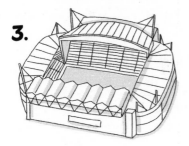

2.

3.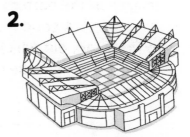

4.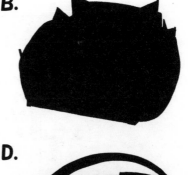

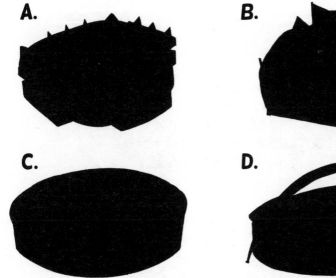

A.

B.

C.

D.

ODD ONE OUT

Each list has an entry that is the odd one out.
Can you figure it out? Read the clues
above each question to help you.

1. CLUE: He once managed the Nagoya Grampus club in Japan.

ARSÈNE WENGER

PEP GUARDIOLA

ALEX FERGUSON

ZINEDINE ZIDANE

2. CLUE: Former Manchester City star Vincent Kompany
became this club's player-manager in 2019.

PSV EINDHOVEN

FEYENOORD

ANDERLECHT

AFC AJAX

3. CLUE: The Women's World Cup
hosts but never winners.

NORWAY

CHINA

GERMANY

JAPAN

4. CLUE: The club's symbol is a cockerel.

LEICESTER CITY

TOTTENHAM HOTSPUR

MANCHESTER UNITED

BLACKBURN ROVERS

5. CLUE: Only one of these teams could have looked forward to promotion in 2018–2019.

YEOVIL TOWN

BRISTOL CITY

MILLWALL LIONESSES

CHELSEA

6. CLUE: Who doesn't appear on the pitch with a whistle?

ANDRE GRAY

LEE MASON

ANDRE MARRINER

MICHAEL OLIVER

BRITISH FOOTBALL TEAMS

Can you find these British football teams in this wordsearch grid? Which team do you support?

```
M A N C H E S T E R U N I T E D V S W
A B R I A H T O N H B V E A L B I O N
N H U D D E R S F I E L D T O W N M Z
C I R Z Q H H Q E H L E N F U L H A M
H L V J E C P V Z A T P U B R S A K M
E T D E D M J W N I H K I W T X F W C
S L G T O T T E N H A M H O T S P U R
T E U Z A I S U E V E R T O N V C A L
E I F W V R M E K V W C T Y Y O D O N
R C W C A A F I A W W Z W E K H R V Q
C E T L H C G E F A Z Y S I A G B K G
I S B T P A S O U T H A M P T O N W B
T T S O S L Y T X F G K Y X K H I U O
Y E Y I E A F C B O U R N E M O U T H
W R Y H N M V C A R D I F F C I T Y G
M C C D N Y E H H D L I V E R P O O L
V I N E W C A S T L E U N I T E D B Q
Y T K F V X C R Y S T A L P A L A C E
H Y G I B F N X G O F B U R N L E Y G
```

AFC BOURNEMOUTH
ALBION
ARSENAL
BURNLEY
CARDIFF CITY
CHELSEA
CRYSTAL PALACE
EVERTON
FULHAM
HUDDERSFIELD TOWN

LEICESTER CITY
LIVERPOOL
MANCHESTER CITY
MANCHESTER UNITED
NEWCASTLE UNITED
SOUTHAMPTON
TOTTENHAM HOTSPUR
WATFORD
WEST HAM UNITED

WE ARE THE CHAMPIONS!

This football team is celebrating a win. Can you work out which piece of the jigsaw is missing?

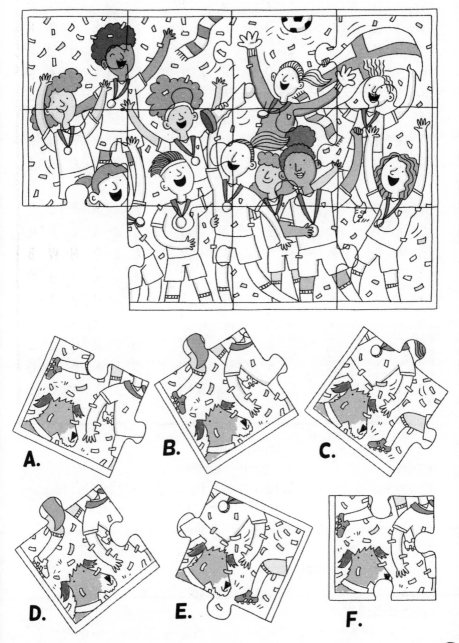

A.

B.

C.

D.

E.

F.

CROSSWORD

Put your knowledge of all things football
to the test by completing this crossword.

ACROSS

3. Nationality of Neymar **(9)**
4. Winning team of the most
league titles in England **(10,6)**
7. Anagram (clue: position
on the pitch): KIRTSRE **(7)**

DOWN

1. Portuguese attacker; plays
for Italian club Juventus **(9,7)**
2. England's home stadium **(7)**
5. Pass played across
the pitch **(5)**
6. Take the ball from
an opponent **(6)**
8. Colour of Manchester
United's home shirts **(3)**

MATCH DAY MEMORY

Study the picture below, then cover it up and
answer the questions on the next page.

MATCH DAY MEMORY

Once you've studied the picture on the previous page, answer the questions below (without peeking!).

1. How many people are in the picture?

2. How many fans are queuing for tickets?

3. What three food items is the van selling?

4. How many flags are in the picture?

5. How many animals are in the picture?

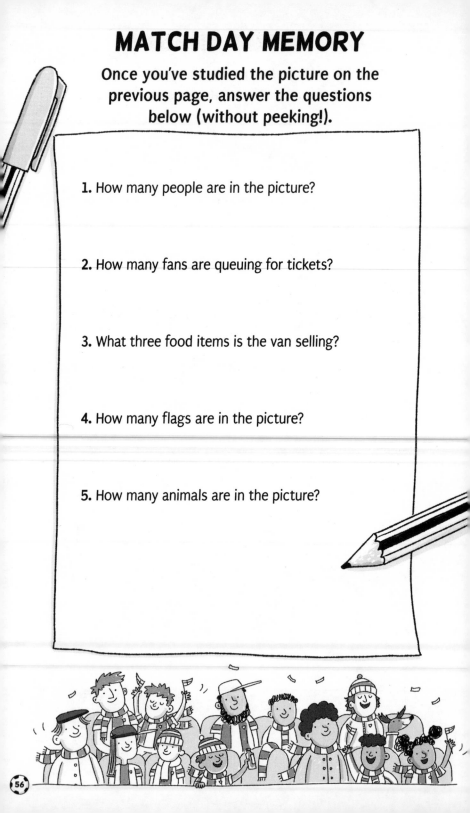

Connect the dots to reveal a
Premier League club crest.

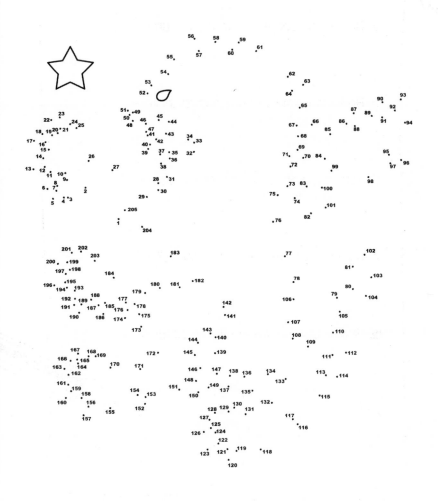

WOMEN'S WORLD CUP QUIZ

Unscramble the letters to reveal the correct answer to each question about the Women's World Cup.

1. Which country hosted the first Women's World Cup in 1991?

INCHA

— — — — —

2. Which South American footballer has scored more Women's World Cup goals than any other player?

ATRAM

— — — — —

3. Who scored five goals in a single game at the 2019 Women's World Cup?

ELAX GAMRON

— — — —   — — — — — —

4. Which team lost to Germany 11-0 at the 2007 Women's World Cup?

EATINGRAN

— — — — — — — — —

5. Which team is the only side to have won the Women's World Cup four times?

DUNEIT TASSET

— — — — — —   — — — — —

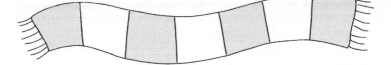

6. Which Brazilian footballer is the only player to have appeared at seven Women's World Cup tournaments?

RAMGFIO

— — — — — — —

7. Who captained England at the 2019 Women's World Cup?

PTHES OHUHTONG

— — — — — — — — — — — —

8. Which US football star has played in more Women's World Cup matches than any other player?

NESTRIKI ILYLL

— — — — — — — — — —

9. Which England player was the joint leading scorer at the 2019 Women's World Cup with six goals?

NELLE THIWE

— — — — — — — —

10. Which team, apart from the United States, are the only team to have won two Women's World Cups in a row?

ANGRYME

— — — — — — —

STADIUMS

Can you find these football stadiums in this wordsearch grid? Do you know which clubs they belong to?

```
S A N T I A G O B E R N A B E U V H L
E C Y C N S O H P N N X B L K P L D M
B A J J Z N N U B O G D W B A P E Y T
X O L Y M P I A S T A D I O N Z M I B
E W L M K G I X B L U Z H N I K I C L
W E S T A D I O D A L U Z C Q Z R A V
D B K O X R Y J R Q C F O S S B A I K
S R C K P P A K D R P N L S T B T Z B
C A M P N O U C T Y K T D T A Y E H L
E R N E Z K L Q A D W K T J D C S W U
B E X S S K Y I W N G K R A E C O P E
T Q R M I T D L A W A G A M D B A F H
P E K P L R A G N A T Q F E E W C J R
H V V V V Y O L H F O Y F S F E F H R
H J G X T A K V L P R A O P R M R A F
B J F N N R N F S A K R R A A B Y X D
F R I E N D S A R E N A D R N L N B U
N C W U L V G L N V X U D K C E I P U
R B U C V O S V P A R K E N E Y Y M T
```

CAMP NOU

EMIRATES

ESTADIO DA LUZ

FRIENDS ARENA

LUZHNIKI

MARACANA

MESTALLA

OLD TRAFFORD

OLYMPIASTADION

PARKEN

ROSE BOWL

SAN SIRO

SANTIAGO BERNABEU

STADE DE FRANCE

ST JAMES' PARK

WEMBLEY

END OF SEASON PHOTOSHOOT

Study these two photoshoots carefully – can you find eight differences between them?

TRUE OR FALSE?

Did you know that the FA Cup is the oldest football competition in the world? Put your knowledge of it to the test by picking out which of these statements are true and which are false.

1. The first FA Cup Final in 1872 was held at a cricket ground, the Kennington Oval.

True ☐   False ☐

2. Every FA Cup winning team has come from England.

True ☐   False ☐

3. The fastest ever FA Cup goal was scored in 2001, after only four seconds.

True ☐   False ☐

4. Manchester United have lost eight FA Cup finals.

True ☐   False ☐

5. Chelsea have won the FA Cup more times than any other team.

True ☐   False ☐

6. Wigan Athletic had only one shot on target in the 2013 FA Cup final, but they still beat Manchester City.

True ☐   False ☐

7. Tottenham Hotspur are the only non-league team to have won the FA Cup.

True ☐   False ☐

8. No Scottish team has ever appeared in an FA Cup final.

True ☐   False ☐

9. The Royal Engineers football club were the first team to appear in three FA Cup finals, in 1872, 1874 and 1875.

True ☐   False ☐

10. Wayne Rooney scored the fastest ever FA Cup final goal.

True ☐   False ☐

PENALTY SHOOTOUT

Can you take your team to goal-scoring glory by only kicking balls that contain multiples of 7 and are next to each other? You can move diagonally.

4	16	2	56	33	16
16	11	7	12	13	10
10	5	11	7	14	45
16	12	42	4	3	14
2	1	28	36	16	1
4	11	6	7	8	10

START

GOAL SCORERS

Can you find these top male goal scorers in this wordsearch grid?

```
C F E R E N C P U S K A S L D R I S K
R G M I R O S L A V K L O S E L O R O
I O G V I U S H L O W Y B S N Z K O T
S D G N F S F I U G X A V U P O U B A
T F U N C T D J I S U J A S Y P N B R
I R X J G H J B S T X D M X O V I I G
A E C U Q I J J S E P K X U K H S E E
N Y G Z I E B L U R M D H Q P S H K S
O C R K L R C P A N C O L C E S I E Q
R H V M O R X Y R J D P R M D L G A R
O I R Z Z Y K D E O R K L L A V E N M
N T R O P H X M Z H R E A M V E K E W
A A G E K E O C S N N H A L I D A E I
L L W A Y N E R O O N E Y V D U M T Y
D U U T E R C R I P Z S M A V G A B V
O D O G G Y E L P E D A Y W I W M L U
R O B I N V A N P E R S I E L Y O A N
B A S H A R A B D U L L A H L J T X S
B G E N N W I K Q T N E I Q A S O E I
```

ALI DAEI

BASHAR ABDULLAH

CRISTIANO RONALDO

DAVID VILLA

FERENC PUSKAS

GODFREY CHITALU

KUNISHIGE KAMAMOTO

LIONEL MESSI

LUIS SUAREZ

MIROSLAV KLOSE

PELÉ

STERN JOHN

ROBBIE KEANE

ROBIN VAN PERSIE

THIERRY HENRY

WAYNE ROONEY

CROSSWORD

Put your knowledge of all things football to the test by completing this crossword.

ACROSS

3. Winner of the 2017–2018 Premier League **(10,4)**

5. Colour of Chelsea's home kit **(4)**

6. Anagram (clue: leader of the team): TPACNAI **(7)**

7. Played in four World Cups, and his Brazilian team won three **(4)**

DOWN

1. Argentine footballer; captains Barcelona **(6,5)**

2. Liverpool player; won the 2018–2019 Premier League Golden Glove award **(7,6)**

4. Replacement on the pitch **(10)**

SOCK JUMBLE

These football socks have got mixed up in the wash.
Can you match them into identical pairs?

FOOTIE HALL OF FAME

Europe is home to some legendary clubs and equally great players who have made it into the hall of fame. Can you score highly in this multiple choice quiz?

1. Which team has won the UEFA Champions League 13 times, more than any other side?

a) AC Milan

b) Juventus

c) Barcelona

d) Real Madrid

2. Which French team has won more league titles than any other team?

a) Saint Etienne

b) Bordeaux

c) Paris Saint-Germain

d) Marseille

3. Which team has won the Bundesliga (Germany's top league) more times than any other?

a) Borussia Dortmund

b) Schalke

c) Bayern Munich

d) Hamburg

4. Which player has won the European Golden Boot five times for scoring more goals in a season than any other player?

a) Luis Suárez

b) Cristiano Ronaldo

c) Neymar

d) Lionel Messi

5. Which French club has appeared in more Champions League competitions than any other?

    a) Lyon   c) Paris Saint-Germain

    b) Marseille   d) Monaco

6. Which was the first British team to win the European Cup or UEFA Champions League?

a) Manchester United   c) Celtic

    b) Liverpool   d) Nottingham Forest

7. Which player held the world record transfer fee for a goalkeeper in 2001, and in 2019 was still playing in a top European league?

a) Iker Casillas   c) Petr Cech

b) Gianluigi Buffon   d) David de Gea

8. Which Italian city is home to clubs who have won Serie A (Italy league championship) the most times in total?

    a) Rome   c) Turin

    b) Napoli   d) Milan

9. Which legendary player scored over 510 goals in the Hungarian and Spanish leagues, and won the European Cup three times?

a) Ferenc Puskás   c) Eusebio

b) Johan Cruyff   d) Zinedine Zidane

GOAL SCORE MATCH UP

All these teams or players have had record runs where they simply couldn't stop scoring. Can you match the correct team or player to their super statistic?

Brazil

Cristiano Ronaldo

Arsenal

Jamie Vardy

Lionel Messi

Norway

Real Madrid

Just Fontaine

6 FIFA World Cup games in a row

11 UEFA Champions League games in a row

15 Women's World Cup games in a row

21 Spanish League games in a row

11 Premier League games in a row

73 games in a row

55 league games in a row

18 FIFA World Cup games in a row

COMPLEX CUBE

Imagine cutting out and folding up the picture below to make a cube. Which one of the four images at the bottom of the page would match that cube? A good way to tackle this puzzle is to first work out which cubes are clearly wrong. The remaining cube must be the correct one.

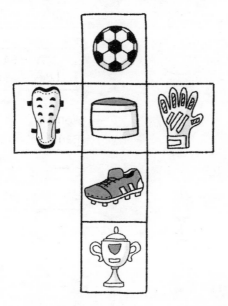

A.

B.

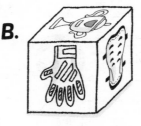

C.

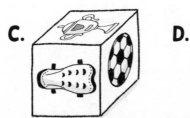

D.

GAMING GRID

Follow the footballs in the order shown at the top of the console to get from start to finish. You can move across, up, and down but not diagonally.

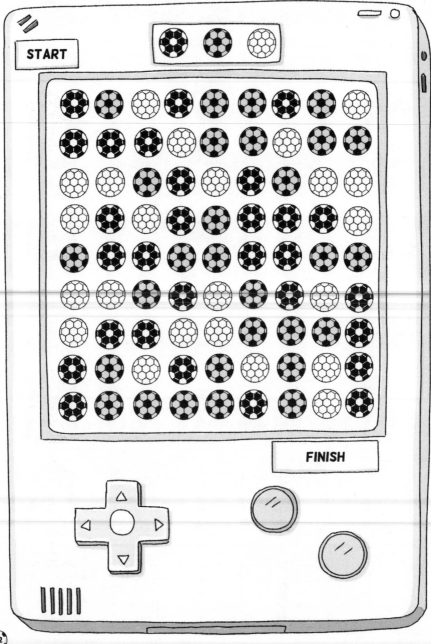

ODD TROPHY OUT
Can you find three trophies in this collection
that look different to the rest?

SUPER SCORERS

Can you find these top female goal scorers in this wordsearch grid?

```
A O Z P A T R I Z I A P A N C I O Z G
B P B C S C A R O L I N A M O R A C E
B M T H H I I A Z J X X Z U E E J T L
Y G B R E X G B D C T N N A S O U I I
W W W I B E Q Q C O I W I I L X L F S
A M L S Q T H L C R V U D K U T I F A
M I R T A O Z Y P H F O K A O F E E B
B C Y I Z S P T E G M D G Y X Z F N E
A H S N R R I J A A J Q L K Y L L Y T
C E J E O G E E I C K I C L T L E M T
H L J S R D S T N D L N D P J C E I A
F L Q I F M R A B E W D M B S A T L V
O E B N D O U T N M D U V M U R I B I
S A J C P D W I X S U J M Y N I N R N
B K R L N F T P E L X A E R W L G E G
J E J A V S P W R V H Y T W E L H T O
R R H I I N T N O A B D B P N O I T T
B S R R Y Q C K I M U Q E K K Y V R T
X T K G B A O M A R T A Z Y J D K R O
```

ABBY WAMBACH

BIRGIT PRINZ

CARI LLOYD

CAROLINA MORACE

CHRISTINE SINCLAIR

ELISABETTA VINGOTTO

HAN DUAN

JULIE FLEETING

KRISTINE LILY

MARTA

MIA HAMM

MICHELLE AKERS

PATRIZIA PANCIO

PORTIA MODISE

SUN WEN

TIFFENY MILBRETT

TRANSFER DAY

Transfer occurs when a player moves from one club to another for a fee. Can you match the correct player to their club and transfer fee?

Dele Alli

Paul Pogba

Ian Wright

Luis Suarez

Fran Kirby

Robert Lewandowski

Mohamed Salah

Jamie Vardy

Crystal Palace
for gym equipment

Leicester City
for £1 million

Tottenham
for £5 million

Bayern Munich
for free

Liverpool
for £34 million

Manchester United
for £89 million

Chelsea
for £50,000

Barcelona
for £65 million

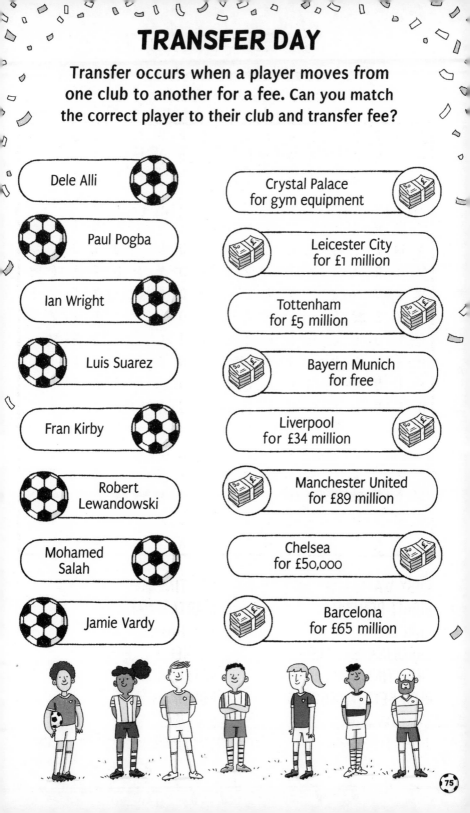

TEAM SCRAMBLE

Unscramble the anagrams to reveal
the international football teams.

1. OBAAELRCN

_ _ _ _ _ _ _ _ _

2. PAAILRSME

_ _ _ _ _ _ _ _ _

3. RIERV PATLE

_ _ _ _ _   _ _ _ _ _

4. MCHATENESR CYIT

_ _ _ _ _ _ _ _ _ _
_ _ _ _

5. LILVORPEO

_ _ _ _ _ _ _ _ _

6. ELINVCAA

_ _ _ _ _ _ _ _

7. RAEL MDIADR

_ _ _ _   _ _ _ _ _ _

8. HCAESEL

_ _ _ _ _ _ _

9. AEYBNR MCUIHN

_ _ _ _ _ _   _ _ _ _ _ _

10. LASNAER

_ _ _ _ _ _ _

KEEPY-UPPIES

Can you match each of these players with their silhouette?

A.

B.

C.

D.

E.

F.

1.

2.

3.

4.

5.

6.

GOLDEN GOALIES

Can you find these goalkeepers in this wordsearch grid?

```
A G I A N L U I G I B U F F O N C H M
Z L T H I B A U T C O U R T O I S I R
W J I Q U J A N O B L A K C T C M Z A
G V P S N E D W I N V A N D E R S A R
R D A J S W A S M F C A P Y K X V A K
I T V O E O B S F V A J H Z T I V D J
S L C R D U N Q J D I N O Z O F F A S
G O R D O N B A N K S J P S V L X V A
D R A A F W S Z I R K L E X M E S I R
X Q E N L Y S K S A J K S N A V A D A
X I X P S W X L C Q Q J O E N Y A D H
T A Z I F L C Z X E L L O U A J E B
J G I C J Z F D U F E X O L E S C G O
J I I K E R C A S I L L A S L H C E U
K X R F S I A D E B R Y F W N I W A H
K X J O E R I N M C L E O D E N R Q A
V T M R L R Z P H P N K H G U C U L D
A N P D P Y X W J V A B D E E O X D D
K A R E N B A R D S L E Y A R T K W I
```

ALISSON

DAVID DE GEA

DINO ZOFF

ERIN MCLEOD

EDWIN VAN DER SAR

GIANLUIGI BUFFON

GORDON BANKS

HOPE SOLO

IKER CASILLAS

JAN OBLAK

JORDAN PICKFORD

KAREN BARDSLEY

LEV YASHIN

MANUEL NEUER

SARAH BOUHADDI

THIBAUT COURTOIS

ODD FOOTBALL OUT

Spot three footballs that look different to the others.

CROSSWORD

Put your knowledge of all things football
to the test by completing this crossword.

ACROSS

6. Welsh football player known for his fierce left foot **(6,4)**

7. Club whose fans are called Villans **(5,5)**

8. Retired from England duty in 2017 with 53 goals in 119 international appearances **(5,6)**

DOWN

1. Professional association football league in Germany **(10)**

2. Zinedine Zidane was sent off for this aggressive foul **(8)**

3. Portuguese 'Coach of the Century' in 2015 **(4,8)**

4. Anagram (clue: prevents the ball going in the goal): EEREPLKOAG **(10)**

5. When any player other than the goalkeeper handles the ball **(8)**

MANAGER MIX-UP

Unscramble the anagrams to
reveal the football managers.

1. JSOE IMURNHOO

_ _ _ _
_ _ _ _ _ _ _ _

2. LAEX EGUSORNF

_ _ _ _
_ _ _ _ _ _ _ _

3. ASENRE NWEGER

_ _ _ _ _ _
_ _ _ _ _ _

4. EPP GULAARDIO

_ _ _
_ _ _ _ _ _ _ _ _

5. JGENUR KLPPO

_ _ _ _ _ _
_ _ _ _ _ _

6. CRLAO ATTENCLOI

_ _ _ _ _
_ _ _ _ _ _ _ _

7. RFAAEL BITEZEN

_ _ _ _ _ _
_ _ _ _ _ _

8. NATNOIO NCOTE

_ _ _ _ _ _
_ _ _ _ _

9. OULIS AVN ALGA

_ _ _ _ _ _ _ _ _
_ _ _ _

10. JGORE SAAOLIMP

_ _ _ _ _
_ _ _ _ _ _ _ _

TRANSFER FEES

Transfer occurs when a player moves from one club to another for a fee. Can you match the correct player to their record-breaking transfer fee?

1. The most expensive defender, bought for £75 million in 2018.

_ _ _ _ _ _   _ _ _   _ _ _ _

2. The world record transfer, bought by Paris Saint-Germain for £198 million.

_ _ _ _ _ _

3. The most expensive British footballer, bought by Real Madrid for £86 million.

_ _ _ _ _ _   _ _ _ _

4. The first player to be transferred twice for more than £75 million each time.

_ _ _ _ _ _ _ _ _

_ _ _ _ _ _ _

5. The world's most expensive goalkeeper, bought for £71.6 million.

_ _ _ _   _ _ _ _ _ _ _ _ _

GARETH BALE   NEYMAR

KEPA ARRIZABALAGA   CRISTIANO RONALDO

VIRGIL VAN DIJK

VICTORY PARADE

Can you spot eight differences
between these two victory parades?

WOMEN'S WORLD CUP QUIZ

It's time to test your knowledge of women's international football! Can you find the correct answer to the questions below?

1. Which US player scored the most goals at a single Women's World Cup tournament?
a) Mia Hamm
b) Carli Lloyd
c) Michelle Akers
d) Alex Morgan

2. Amandine Henry captained her team in the first 2019 Women's World Cup game. Which team did she play for?
a) France
b) Italy
c) USA
d) The Netherlands

3. Which member of England's 2019 Women's World Cup squad has played the most games for her country?
a) Lucy Bronze
b) Jill Scott
c) Toni Duggan
d) Karen Carney

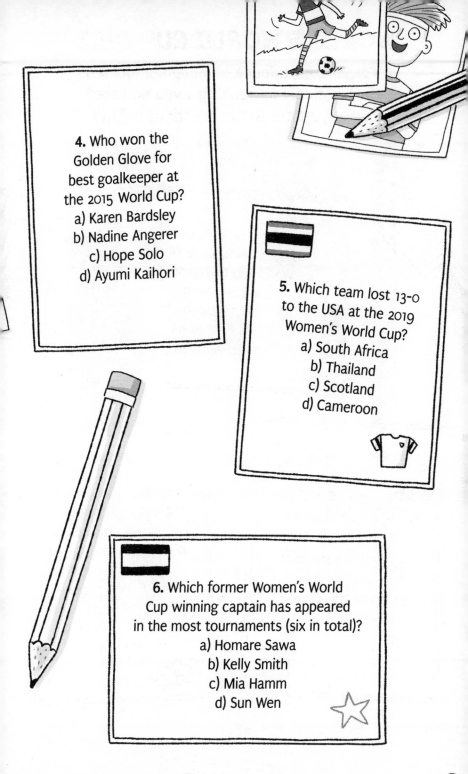

4. Who won the Golden Glove for best goalkeeper at the 2015 World Cup?
a) Karen Bardsley
b) Nadine Angerer
c) Hope Solo
d) Ayumi Kaihori

5. Which team lost 13-0 to the USA at the 2019 Women's World Cup?
a) South Africa
b) Thailand
c) Scotland
d) Cameroon

6. Which former Women's World Cup winning captain has appeared in the most tournaments (six in total)?
a) Homare Sawa
b) Kelly Smith
c) Mia Hamm
d) Sun Wen

CROSSWORD

Put your knowledge of all things football
to the test by completing this crossword.

ACROSS

3. Nationality of Cristiano Ronaldo **(10)**

6. Position that protects a team's goal **(8)**

8. English football club; The Canaries **(7,4)**

DOWN

1. Ex-manager of Spurs, Birmingham City and West Ham **(5,8)**

2. An unfair play **(4)**

4. Manchester United's nickname **(3,6)**

5. Anagram (clue: controls the game): EERFEER **(7)**

7. Liverpool's home stadium **(7)**

MATCH TICKET MAZE

Starting at the top of the maze, find a sneaky way through this ticket queue.

MYSTERY CREST

Connect the dots to reveal a Premier League club crest.

WORLD CUP HOSTS

Can you find these countries who have hosted the men's and women's World Cup in this wordsearch grid?

```
C H I L E N X Z W H O J A P A N A D K
F X A B G W S G O Q P R O I R V E F Q
T Z L P P N W C X N Z J S C T A N W I
K W V P M Q I T P D H S W F A U G X V
X L Z Y K X T J D B U I J B P N L J R
S T I W E P Z B D R P Y G N J A A W Q
H J B M X O E U G R A B Y Y Y L N D L
Q P O Z P J R N Q N N B B C C S D P A
B P R E U L L I I I O T P S C V U F Z
R C T R I J A T Q X J R C V A P W J R
V F V Z K B N E N B U R U G U A Y M P
S P A I N E D D X R B T I V O M D F S
V R X J G Y L S V P E D F H N Y G D W
B M X R C H Q T D Z Q C H E N F E I E
K I A Q H C J A R X U U A U W M R T D
W V P N I L B T F M L V T Y K S M A E
T C S L N Q I E P X J U S F A I A L N
M P F V A A A S I C P M O Z O C N Y E
V L U X J Z F X P E B M C D R U Y R O
```

ARGENTINA
BRAZIL
CANADA
CHILE
CHINA
ENGLAND
GERMANY
ITALY

JAPAN
MEXICO
RUSSIA
SPAIN
SWEDEN
SWITZERLAND
UNITED STATES
URUGUAY

OUT OF ORDER

All of these footie-themed lists are in the wrong order.
Can you put them in the right order by following
the instructions above each one?

1. Place these five teams in order of the most
seasons in which they finished winners or
runners-up in the Scottish league.

Hibernian

Rangers

Heart of Midlothian

Celtic

Aberdeen

2. Place these five England stars in order
of who made their England debut first.

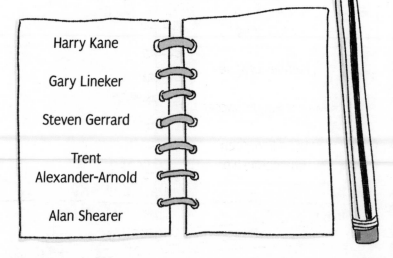

Harry Kane

Gary Lineker

Steven Gerrard

Trent
Alexander-Arnold

Alan Shearer

3. Place these five English clubs in order of how many league championships they have won.

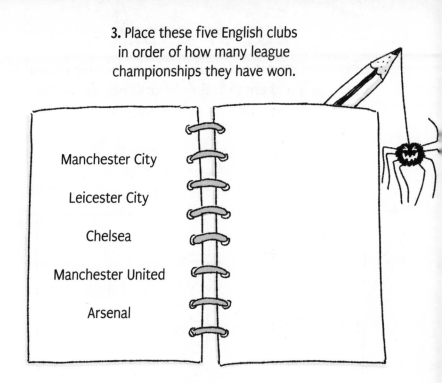

Manchester City

Leicester City

Chelsea

Manchester United

Arsenal

4. Place these five competitions in order of which began earliest.

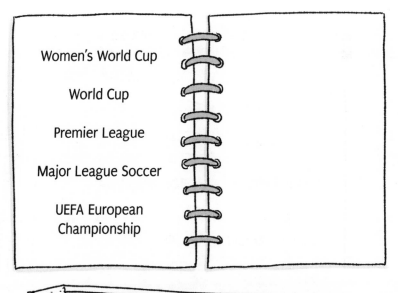

Women's World Cup

World Cup

Premier League

Major League Soccer

UEFA European Championship

STADIUM SCRAMBLE

Unscramble the anagrams to reveal
the stadiums. Can you name the
teams they belong to?

1. SAANGTOI AEUBNBER

_ _ _ _ _ _ _ _

_ _ _ _ _ _ _ _

2. ADETSIO AD LZU

_ _ _ _ _ _ _

_ _ _ _ _

3. CCETLI PKRA

_ _ _ _ _ _

_ _ _ _

4. UUSVJNET

_ _ _ _ _ _ _

5. EADISTO NNATEIOCER

_ _ _ _ _ _

_ _ _ _ _ _ _ _ _

6. ACPM NUO

_ _ _ _ _ _ _

7. SLGIAN INUDA APKR

_ _ _ _ _ _

_ _ _ _ _ _ _ _

8. ODL TRRFOAFD

_ _ _

_ _ _ _ _ _ _

9. TEH MRAAAACN

_ _ _

_ _ _ _ _ _ _ _

10. WEEBLYM

_ _ _ _ _ _ _

BOOT MUDDLE

These football boots are all mixed up.
Can you match up the identical pairs?

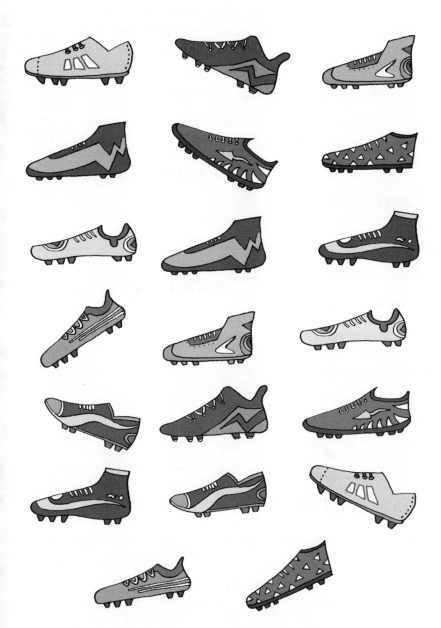

STADIUM STATS

Each stadium listed below hosted a game which had an attendance record. Can you match the stadium with its record-smashing game?

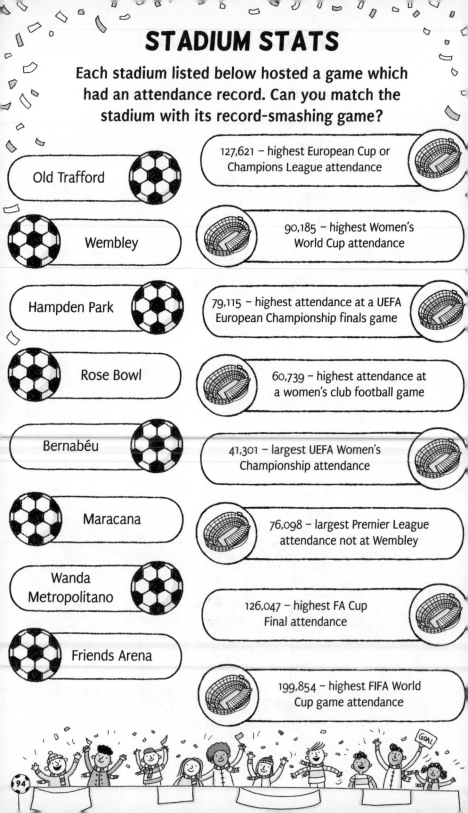

Old Trafford

127,621 – highest European Cup or Champions League attendance

Wembley

90,185 – highest Women's World Cup attendance

Hampden Park

79,115 – highest attendance at a UEFA European Championship finals game

Rose Bowl

60,739 – highest attendance at a women's club football game

Bernabéu

41,301 – largest UEFA Women's Championship attendance

Maracana

76,098 – largest Premier League attendance not at Wembley

Wanda Metropolitano

126,047 – highest FA Cup Final attendance

Friends Arena

199,854 – highest FIFA World Cup game attendance

AWESOME ANTHEM

Spot eight differences between these two photographs of teams singing their anthems.

FOOTBALL JOKES: SECOND HALF

What runs along the edge of the pitch but never moves?

The sideline.

Football Fan 1: "Why can't my football team host a good tea party?"

Football Fan 2: "Is it because they've got no cups?"

Why are pigs rubbish at playing in a football team?

Because they always hog the ball.

Which football side did Shy Sarah and Very Quiet Veronica play for?

The reserve-d team.

Why did the defender turn up to the match with a sketchpad and colouring pencils?

He was hoping to draw the game.

Which goalkeepers can jump higher than a crossbar?

All of them, as crossbars can't jump.

What did the polite footballer say when he accidentally burped during a game?

"I'm so sorry, it was a freak hic!"

Why was the chicken sent off the pitch?

For fowl play.

What is a referee's favourite drink?

A cup of penal-tea.

What happened to the football team who ate trifle before every league game?

They got jelly-gated.

JUMBLED BOTTLES

How many bottles are jumbled up below?

TACTICAL MAZE

This football manager is explaining tactics to his team. Can you make it through the maze to reach the goal?

CROSSWORD

Put your knowledge of all things football
to the test by completing this crossword.

ACROSS

2. Oldest international
continental football
competition **(4,7)**

4. Nickname is
'Egyptian Messi' **(7,5)**

6. When a player accidentally
kicks the ball into
their net **(3,4)**

DOWN

1. Anagram (clue: position on
the pitch): FIMDEIDLRE **(10)**

2. Barcelona's home
stadium **(4,3)**

3. Manager for Manchester
United between 1986
and 2013 **(4,8)**

5. Bird on the Brighton
& Hove Albion logo **(7)**

TICKET TWINS

Draw a line to match each ticket to its partner.

TRUE OR FALSE?

Can you work out which of these
freaky feats and extraordinary events
are true and which ones are false?
Tick the box you think is correct.

1. The transfer fee paid for Norway
striker Kenneth Kristensen in 2003
was 75kg of fresh shrimp.

True ☐   False ☐

2. Liverpool goalkeeper Alisson Becker
has had four number one records
in his home country of Brazil.

True ☐   False ☐

3. Japanese captain Homare Sawa was
given a free island and an aircraft to
fly to it by her country after winning
the 2011 Women's World Cup.

True ☐   False ☐

4. A 2011 match between Claypole and
Victoriano Arenas in Argentina got so out
of hand that the referee showed the red
card 36 times to players, coaches and subs.

True ☐   False ☐

5. Forward Mark Hughes played a match for
Wales in the afternoon and then travelled to
Germany to play for his club the same day.

True ☐   False ☐

6. Manchester City defender Vincent Kompany once scored five goals in a game, but three of them were own goals.

True ☐   False ☐

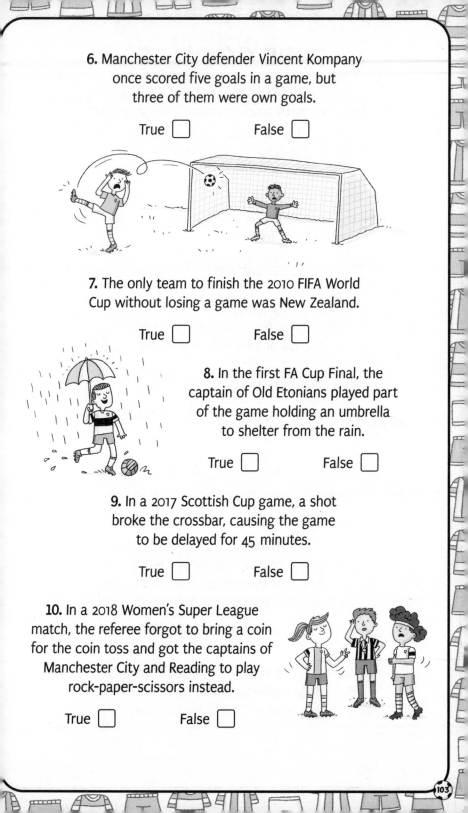

7. The only team to finish the 2010 FIFA World Cup without losing a game was New Zealand.

True ☐   False ☐

8. In the first FA Cup Final, the captain of Old Etonians played part of the game holding an umbrella to shelter from the rain.

True ☐   False ☐

9. In a 2017 Scottish Cup game, a shot broke the crossbar, causing the game to be delayed for 45 minutes.

True ☐   False ☐

10. In a 2018 Women's Super League match, the referee forgot to bring a coin for the coin toss and got the captains of Manchester City and Reading to play rock-paper-scissors instead.

True ☐   False ☐

BOOKED!

Can you solve these referee card number pyramids?
Each card should contain a number that is equal
to the two cards immediately beneath it.

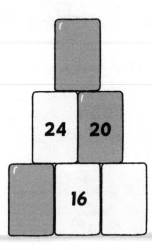

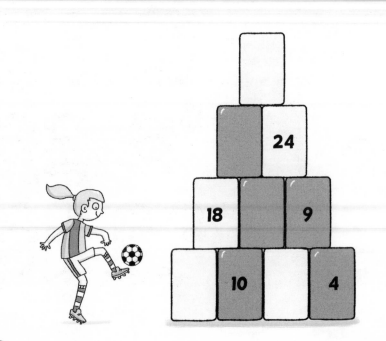

CAR PARK MAZE

This stadium car park is huge – can you find a way through it?

IT'S A GOAL!

Can you take your team to goal-scoring glory by
only kicking balls that contain multiples of 8 and
are next to each other? You can move diagonally.

5	56	12	6	33	9
16	18	24	5	16	4
30	12	32	6	3	45
11	30	42	24	9	13
4	1	3	40	14	31
1	11	6	5	8	9

START

CROSSWORD

Put your knowledge of all things football
to the test by completing this crossword.

ACROSS

2. England goalkeeper for
15 years who won 4 FA Cups
with Arsenal **(5,6)**
5. Italian professional football
club based in Piedmont **(8)**
6. PFA Young Player of
the Year 2019 **(6,8)**
7. Assistant referees that stand
at the edge of the pitch **(8)**
8. Colour of card referees use
to issue a caution **(6)**

DOWN

1. Further period of play
added on to a game if the
scores are equal **(5,4)**
3. Anagram (clue: position
which plays behind defence):
SEEERPW **(7)**
4. Longest-serving
Arsenal manager **(6,6)**

FOOTBALL MAZE

Be quick on your feet and find your
way through this footie maze.

BUILD YOUR DREAM TEAM

It's time to build your dream team.
Pick your favourite players for each
position and fill in the spaces below.

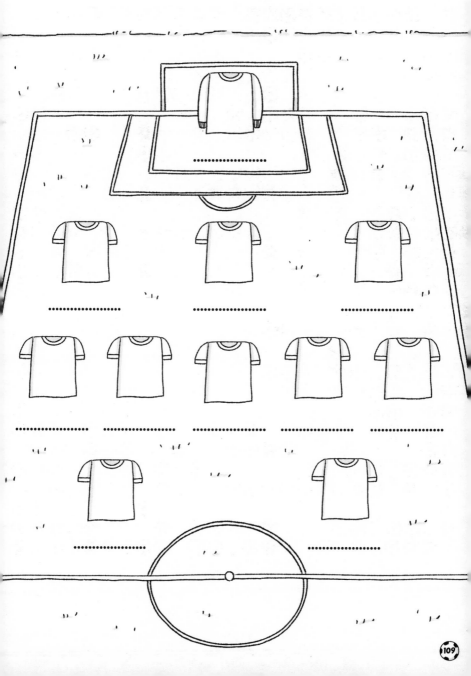

GOING GLOBAL

Every four years, players and fans from around the globe head to the World Cup. Find the correct route through this globe-shaped maze.

FOOTBALL LEGENDS

Can you find these football legends in this wordsearch grid? Who is your favourite?

```
K E L L Y S M I T H A Y B U V H P L A
J S Z R A A G D Y L E E E W A V N M N
J B E K P D J T N K Q H J J U O C A D
H A N N A L J U N G B E R G T G T K R
E O S E H D H A Y P K H K L U D Z X I
Z O L R T S Y C I M C B R B Y U I B Y
P R O N A L D O S A B A Q U M G N J S
F K S N E O L N B R H E W U B K E O H
U J Q H C T D M O C R N Z Z R W D H E
K U C I F A A O Y O V B M G A W I A V
C A Z X A W I B H V K S Q T Q Y N N C
R B B X Y B B Q U A A Z I J N Z E C H
P D D B E O B Q U N C R R J A C Z R E
X F B S B O Z Q U B C U T T S D I U N
R A U N J L C X B A V G Y W U O D Y K
L E V Y A S H I N S W X G E N M A F O
G E O R G E B E S T X V N W D N F P
F R A N Z B E C K E N B A U E R E N I
N C B P U M R U X N C R B Y N K O S W
```

ABBY WAMBACH
ANDRIY SHEVCHENKO
BOBBY CHARLTON
EUSEBIO
FRANZ BECKENBAUER
GEORGE BEST
HANNA LJUNGBERG
JOHAN CRUYFF

KELLY SMITH
LEV YASHIN
MARCO VAN BASTEN
RACHEL YANKEY
RONALDO
SUN WEN
ZICO
ZINEDINE ZIDANE

ANSWERS

TRUE OR FALSE?
PAGE 4-5

1. True
2. False
3. False
4. True
5. True
6. True
7. True
8. False
9. True
10. True

... AND SHE SCORES!
PAGE 6

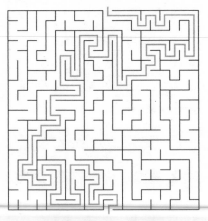

FOOTBALL PYRAMIDS
PAGE 7

WALL BUILDER
PAGE 8-9

GAME ONE

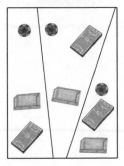

GAME TWO

GAME THREE

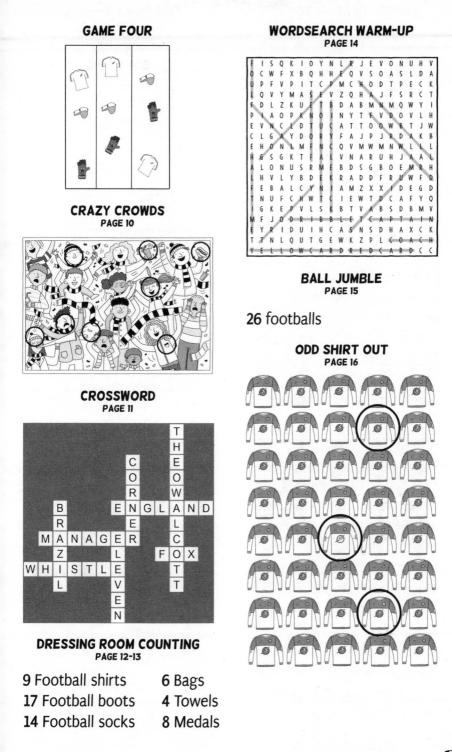

GAME FOUR

WORDSEARCH WARM-UP
PAGE 14

CRAZY CROWDS
PAGE 10

BALL JUMBLE
PAGE 15

26 footballs

CROSSWORD
PAGE 11

ODD SHIRT OUT
PAGE 16

DRESSING ROOM COUNTING
PAGE 12-13

9 Football shirts   **6** Bags
17 Football boots   **4** Towels
14 Football socks   **8** Medals

CLEAN SHEET MATCH UP
PAGE 17

Hope Solo, USA - 102 clean sheets in women's international games (2000-2016)

Joe Hart, England - 46 clean sheets for England in international football (2008-2019)

Peter Shilton, England - 10 clean sheets at the FIFA World Cup, a joint world record (1982-1990)

Gemma Fay, Scotland - Most capped goalkeeper in women's football with 203 games and 32 clean sheets for Scotland (1998-2017)

Iker Casillas, Real Madrid - 59 clean sheets in UEFA Champions League games (1999-2015)

Petr Cech, Chelsea and Arsenal - 202 clean sheets in 443 Premier League games (2004-2018)

Edwin van der Sar, Manchester United - 14 clean sheets in a row in the Premier League (2008-09)

Gianluigi Buffon, Juventus - 53 clean sheets in 123 UEFA Champions League games (2001-2018)

FOOTBALL PHRASES
PAGE 18

1. Back of the net
2. Bicycle kick
3. Clean sheet
4. Dive
5. Dribbling
6. Nutmeg
7. Off the line
8. Extra time
9. Offside
10. Relegation

SCARF SEQUENCES
PAGE 19

A. 120
B. 42
C. 19
D. 13

GUESS THE GOALS
PAGE 20

619 Lionel Messi, Barcelona
450 Cristiano Ronaldo, Real Madrid
221 Robert Lewandowski, Bayern Munich
228 Thierry Henry, Arsenal
216 Ada Hegerberg, Lyon
307 Francesco Totti, Roma
407 Eusebio, Benfica
138 Kris Boyd, Rangers
70 Fara Williams, Everton
111 Marta, UMEÅ IK

PENALTY SHOOTOUT
PAGE 21

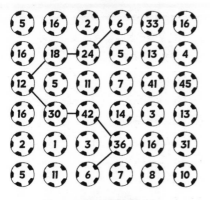

MATCHING CRESTS
PAGE 22-23

GAME ONE

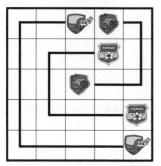

GAME TWO

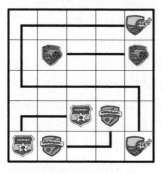

GAME THREE

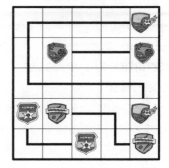

GAME FOUR

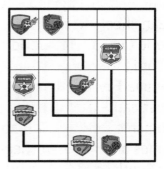

GAME FIVE

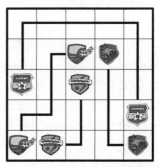

GAME SIX

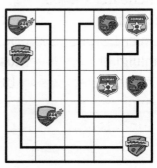

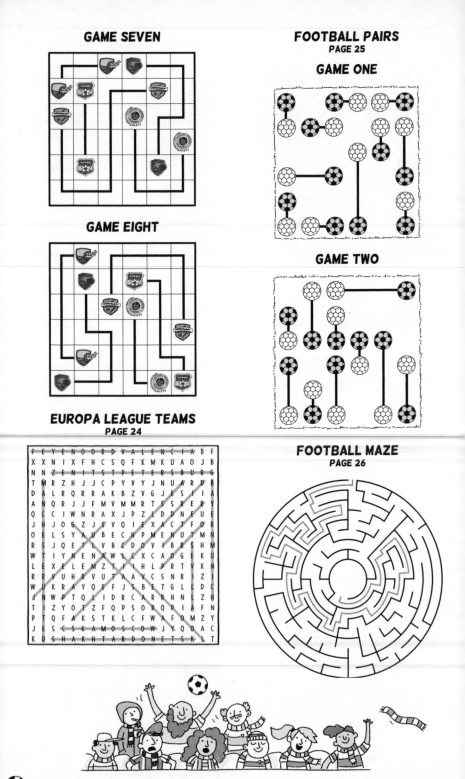

GAME SEVEN

GAME EIGHT

FOOTBALL PAIRS
PAGE 25

GAME ONE

GAME TWO

EUROPA LEAGUE TEAMS
PAGE 24

FOOTBALL MAZE
PAGE 26

CROSSWORD
PAGE 27

CROSSWORD
PAGE 34

WHO AM I?
PAGE 28-29

1. Zinedine Zidane
2. Lucy Bronze
3. Cristiano Ronaldo
4. Jill Scott
5. Jermain Defoe
6. Sergio Aguero
7. Ellen White
8. Gareth Southgate
9. Lothar Matthäus
10. Peter Crouch

BACK OF THE NET
PAGE 32

Ellen scored the goal.

MYSTERY CREST
PAGE 33

Arsenal is the Premier League club crest.

CHAMPIONS LEAGUE TEAMS
PAGE 35

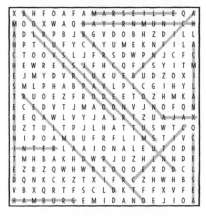

CLUB CONUNDRUM
PAGE 36

Real Madrid - Santiago Bernabéu
Barcelona - Camp Nou
Liverpool - Anfield
Rangers - Ibrox
Bayern Munich - Allianz Arena
Marseille - Stade Velodrome
AC Milan - San Siro
Chelsea - Stamford Bridge

IT'S A GOAL!
PAGE 37

FOOTBALL SHIRT PAIRING
PAGE 41

FOOTBALL LEGENDS QUIZ
PAGE 38-39

1. d	**6.** a
2. b	**7.** d
3. a	**8.** c
4. c	**9.** a
5. b	**10.** d

FOOTIE LEGENDS
PAGE 40

1. Lionel Messi
2. Marta
3. Cristiano Ronaldo
4. Pernille Harder
5. Neymar
6. Wayne Rooney
7. Zinedine Zidane
8. David Beckham
9. Sam Kerr
10. Ada Hegerberg

FOOTIE FACT MATCH UP
PAGE 42-43

1. Gunnersaurus - Arsenal
Harry the Hornet - Watford
Filbert Fox - Leicester City
Hammerhead - West Ham United
Hoopy the Huddle Hound - Celtic
Chirpy Cockerel - Tottenham Hotspur

2. 1930 - Uruguay
1954 - Switzerland
1962 - Chile
1982 - Spain
1994 - USA
2010 - South Africa

3. St. Mark's (West Gorton) - Manchester City
Dial Square - Arsenal
St Domingo - Everton
Thames Ironworks - West Ham

Boscombe St. John's Lads'
Institute FC - AFC
Bournemouth
Newton Heath LYR -
Manchester United

4. 1960 - Soviet Union
1968 - Italy
1988 - Netherlands
2000 - France
2004 - Greece
2016 - Portugal

5. Isobel Christiansen -
England
Rose Lavelle - USA
Lieke Martens -
The Netherlands
Erin Cuthbert - Scotland
Sam Kerr - Australia
Lina Hurtig - Sweden

6. 1872 - Wanderers
1874 - Oxford University
1882 - Old Etonians
1953 - Blackpool
2013 - Wigan Athletic
2019 - Manchester City

NICKNAME SEARCH
PAGE 46

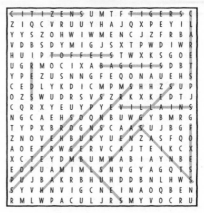

... AND HE SCORES!
PAGE 47

COMPLEX CUBE
PAGE 48

B

STADIUM SILHOUETTES
PAGE 49

1. D

2. A

3. B

4. C

PREMIER LEAGUE QUIZ
PAGE 44-45

1. c	**6.** b
2. b	**7.** c
3. a	**8.** a
4. d	**9.** d
5. b	**10.** b

ODD ONE OUT
PAGE 50-51

1. Arsène Wenger – the others have all won the UEFA Champions League as managers

2. Anderlecht – the others are clubs from the Netherlands whilst Anderlecht are from Belgium

3. China – the only one of the four nations not to have won the FIFA Women's World Cup

4. Tottenham Hotspur – the only team in the list yet to win the Premier League

5. Millwall Lionesses – the only one of the four teams not in the 2018-19 FA Women's Super League

6. Andre Gray - a football striker, the others are Premier League referees

BRITISH FOOTBALL TEAMS
PAGE 52

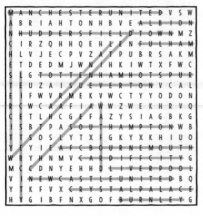

WE ARE THE CHAMPIONS!
PAGE 53

B is the missing jigsaw piece.

CROSSWORD
PAGE 54

MATCH DAY MEMORY
PAGE 55-56

1. 20

2. 4

3. Burgers, hot dogs, fries

4. 12

5. 4 – 1 dog, 3 birds

MYSTERY CREST
PAGE 57

Chelsea is the Premier League club crest.

WOMEN'S WORLD CUP QUIZ
PAGE 58-59

1. China

2. Marta

3. Alex Morgan

4. Argentina

5. United States

6. Formiga

7. Steph Houghton

8. Kristine Lilly

9. Ellen White

10. Germany

STADIUMS
PAGE 60

END OF SEASON PHOTOSHOOT
PAGE 61

TRUE OR FALSE?
PAGE 62-63

1. True	**6.** True
2. False	**7.** True
3. True	**8.** False
4. True	**9.** True
5. False	**10.** False

PENALTY SHOOTOUT
PAGE 64

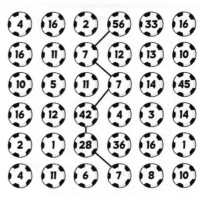

GOAL SCORERS
PAGE 65

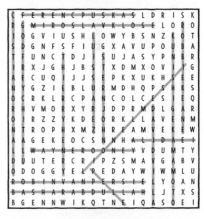

CROSSWORD
PAGE 66

SOCK JUMBLE
PAGE 67

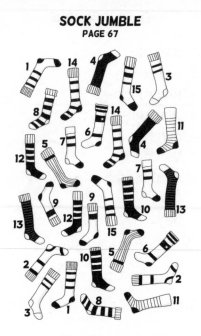

COMPLEX CUBE
PAGE 71

C

GAMING GRID
PAGE 72

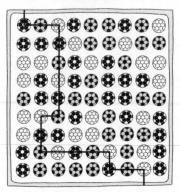

FOOTIE HALL OF FAME
PAGE 68-69

1. d
2. b
3. c
4. d
5. a

6. c
7. b
8. c
9. a

GOAL SCORE MATCH UP
PAGE 70

Brazil - 18 FIFA World Cup games in a row

Cristiano Ronaldo - 11 UEFA Champions League games in a row

Arsenal - 55 league games in a row

Jamie Vardy - 11 Premier League games in a row

Lionel Messi - 21 Spanish League games in a row

Norway - 15 Women's World Cup games in a row

Real Madrid - 73 games in a row

Just Fontaine - 6 FIFA World Cup games in a row

ODD TROPHY OUT
PAGE 73

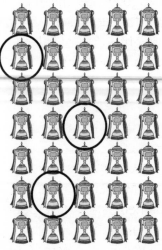

SUPER SCORERS
PAGE 74

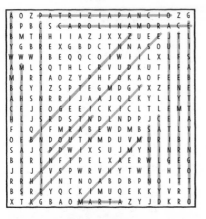

TEAM SCRAMBLE
PAGE 76

1. Barcelona
2. Palmeiras
3. River Plate
4. Manchester City
5. Liverpool
6. Valencia
7. Real Madrid
8. Chelsea
9. Bayern Munich
10. Arsenal

TRANSFER DAY
PAGE 75

Dele Alli - Tottenham
for £5 million
Paul Pogba - Manchester
United for £89 million
Ian Wright - Crystal Palace
for gym equipment
Luis Suarez - Barcelona
for £65 million
Fran Kirby - Chelsea
for £50,000
Robert Lewandowski -
Bayern Munich for free
Mohamed Salah - Liverpool
for £34 million
Jamie Vardy - Leicester City
for £1 million

KEEPY-UPPIES
PAGE 77

1. C   4. B
2. F   5. A
3. E   6. D

GOLDEN GOALIES
PAGE 78

ODD FOOTBALL OUT
PAGE 79

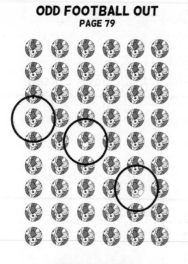

CROSSWORD
PAGE 80

MANAGER MIX-UP
PAGE 81

1. Jose Mourinho
2. Alex Ferguson
3. Arsene Wenger
4. Pep Guardiola
5. Jurgen Klopp
6. Carlo Ancelotti
7. Rafael Benitez
8. Antonio Conte
9. Louis Van Gaal
10. Jorge Sampaoli

TRANSFER FEES
PAGE 82

1. Virgil Van Dijk
2. Neymar
3. Gareth Bale
4. Cristiano Ronaldo
5. Kepa Arrizabalaga

VICTORY PARADE
PAGE 83

WOMEN'S WORLD CUP QUIZ
PAGE 84-85

1. c	4. c
2. a	5. b
3. d	6. a

CROSSWORD
PAGE 86

MATCH TICKET MAZE
PAGE 87

MYSTERY CREST
PAGE 88

Liverpool is the Premier League club crest.

WORLD CUP HOSTS
PAGE 89

```
C H I L E N X Z W H O J A P A N A D K
F X A B G W S G O Q P R O J R V E F Q
T Z L P P N W C X N Z J S C T A N W I
K W V P M Q T P D H S W F A U G X V
X L Z Y K T J D B U I J B P N J R
S T I W E P Z B D R P Y G N J A W Q
H J B M X O E U G R A B Y Y Y L N D L
Q P O Z P J R N Q N N B B C C S D P A
B P R E U L L I O T P S C V U F Z
R C T R I J A T Q X J R C V A P W J R
V F V Z K B M E N B U R U G U A Y M P
S P A I N E D D X R B T I V O M D F S
V R X J G Y L S V P E D F H N Y G D W
B M X R C H Q T D Z Q C H E N F E I E
K I A Q H C J A R X U U A U W M R T D
W V P N I L B T F M L V T Y K S M A E
T C S L N Q I P X J U S F A I I N
M P F V A A A S I C P M O Z O C N Y E
V L U X J Z F X P E B M C D R U Y R O
```

OUT OF ORDER
PAGE 90-91

1. Rangers, Celtic, Aberdeen, Heart of Midlothian, Hibernian
2. Gary Lineker, Alan Shearer, Steven Gerrard, Harry Kane, Trent Alexander-Arnold

3. Manchester United, Chelsea, Manchester City, Arsenal, Leicester City
4. World Cup, UEFA European Championship, Women's World Cup, Premier League, Major League Soccer

STADIUM SCRAMBLE
PAGE 92

1. Santiago Bernabeu
2. Estadio Da Luz
3. Celtic Park
4. Juventus
5. Estadio Centenario
6. Camp Nou
7. Signal Iduna Park
8. Old Trafford
9. The Maracana
10. Wembley

BOOT MUDDLE
PAGE 93

STADIUM STATS
PAGE 94

Old Trafford – 76,098 – largest Premier League attendance not at Wembley
Wembley – 126,047 – highest FA Cup Final attendance
Hampden Park – 127,621 – highest European Cup or Champions League attendance
Rose Bowl – 90,185 – highest Women's World Cup attendance
Bernabéu – 79,115 – highest attendance at a UEFA European Championship finals match
Maracana – 199,854 – highest FIFA World Cup match attendance
Wanda Metropolitano – 60,739 – highest attendance at a women's club football match
Friends Arena – 41,301 – largest UEFA Women's Championship attendance

AWESOME ANTHEM
PAGE 95

JUMBLED BOTTLES
PAGE 98

27 jumbled bottles

TACTICAL MAZE
PAGE 99

CROSSWORD
PAGE 100

BOOKED!
PAGE 104

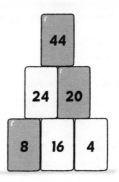

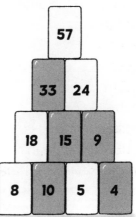

TICKET TWINS
PAGE 101

CAR PARK MAZE
PAGE 105

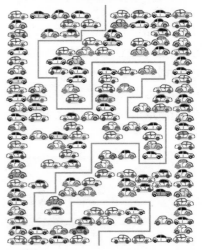

TRUE OR FALSE?
PAGE 102-103

1. True	6. False
2. False	7. True
3. False	8. False
4. True	9. False
5. True	10. True

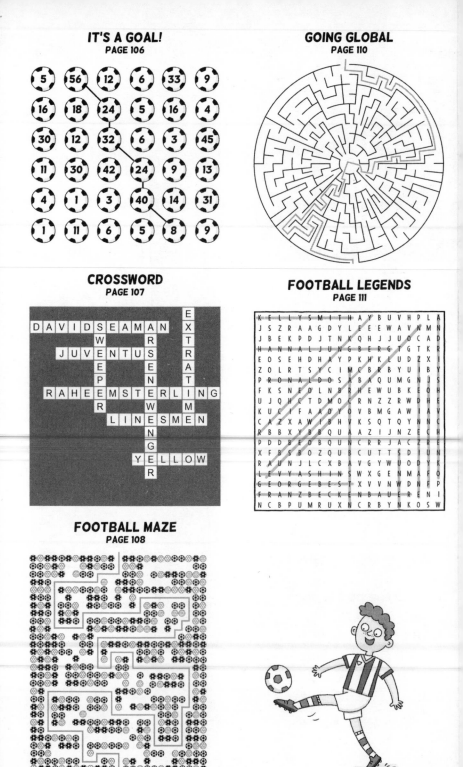

IT'S A GOAL!
PAGE 106

GOING GLOBAL
PAGE 110

CROSSWORD
PAGE 107

DAVIDSEAMAN
JUVENTUS
RAHEEMSTERLING
LINESMEN
EXTRATIME
YELLOW

FOOTBALL LEGENDS
PAGE 111

KELLYSMITH AYBUVHPLA
JSZRAAGDYLEEEWAVNMN
JBEKPDJTNKQHJJUOCAD
HANNALJUNGBERGTGTKR
EOSEHDHAYPKHKLUDZXI
ZOLRTSYCIMCBRBYUIBY
PRONALDOSABAQUMGNJS
FKSNEDLNBRHEWUBKEQH
UJQHCTDMORNZZRWDHE
KUCIFAAOYOVBMGAWIA
CAZXAWIBHVKSQTQYMN
RBBXYBBQUAAZIJNZECH
PDDBEOBQUNCRRJACZRE
XFBSBOZQUBCUTTSDIUN
RAUNJLCXBAVGYWUODY
LEVYASHINSWXGENMAFQ
GEORGEBEST XVVNWDNFP
FRANZBECKENBAUERRENI
NCBPUMRUXNCRBYNKOSW

FOOTBALL MAZE
PAGE 108